DINOSAURS
AND OTHER BEASTLY BEASTS

Illustrated by
Angela Rizza

Written & Edited by Jonny Marx

Consultancy by Dougal Dixon

Designed by Jack Clucas

Cover Design by John Bigwood

BARRON'S

PREHISTORIC TIMELINE

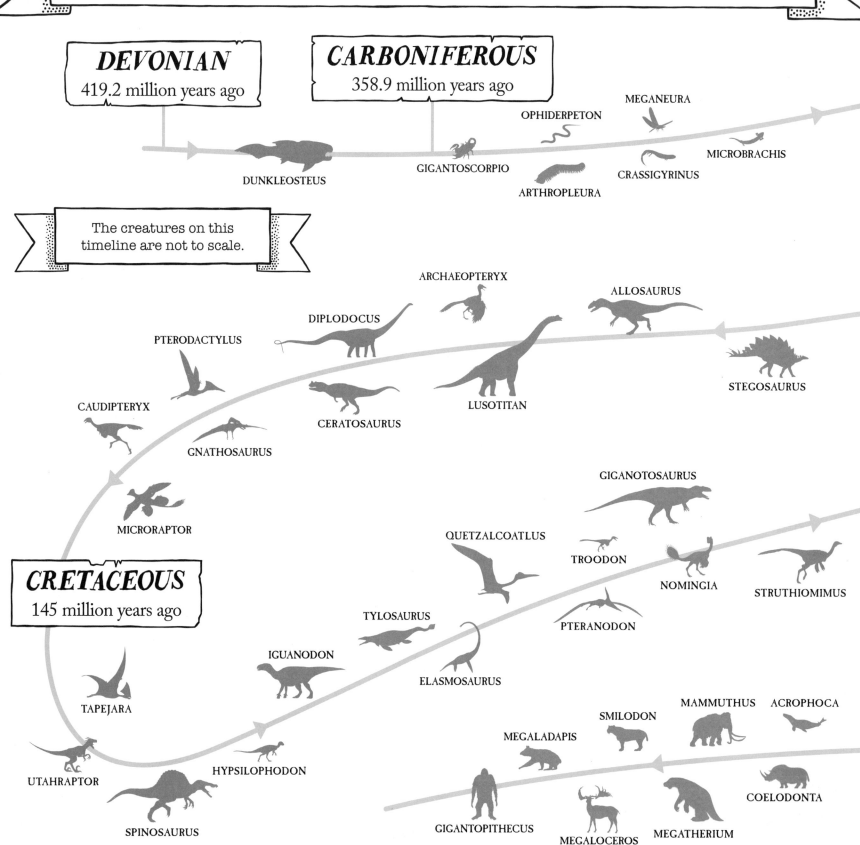

DEVONIAN
419.2 million years ago

CARBONIFEROUS
358.9 million years ago

DUNKLEOSTEUS

GIGANTOSCORPIO

OPHIDERPETON

ARTHROPLEURA

MEGANEURA

CRASSIGYRINUS

MICROBRACHIS

The creatures on this timeline are not to scale.

ARCHAEOPTERYX

DIPLODOCUS

PTERODACTYLUS

ALLOSAURUS

CAUDIPTERYX

GNATHOSAURUS

CERATOSAURUS

LUSOTITAN

STEGOSAURUS

MICRORAPTOR

GIGANOTOSAURUS

QUETZALCOATLUS

TROODON

NOMINGIA

STRUTHIOMIMUS

CRETACEOUS
145 million years ago

TYLOSAURUS

PTERANODON

IGUANODON

ELASMOSAURUS

TAPEJARA

MAMMUTHUS

ACROPHOCA

SMILODON

MEGALADAPIS

UTAHRAPTOR

HYPSILOPHODON

COELODONTA

SPINOSAURUS

GIGANTOPITHECUS

MEGALOCEROS

MEGATHERIUM

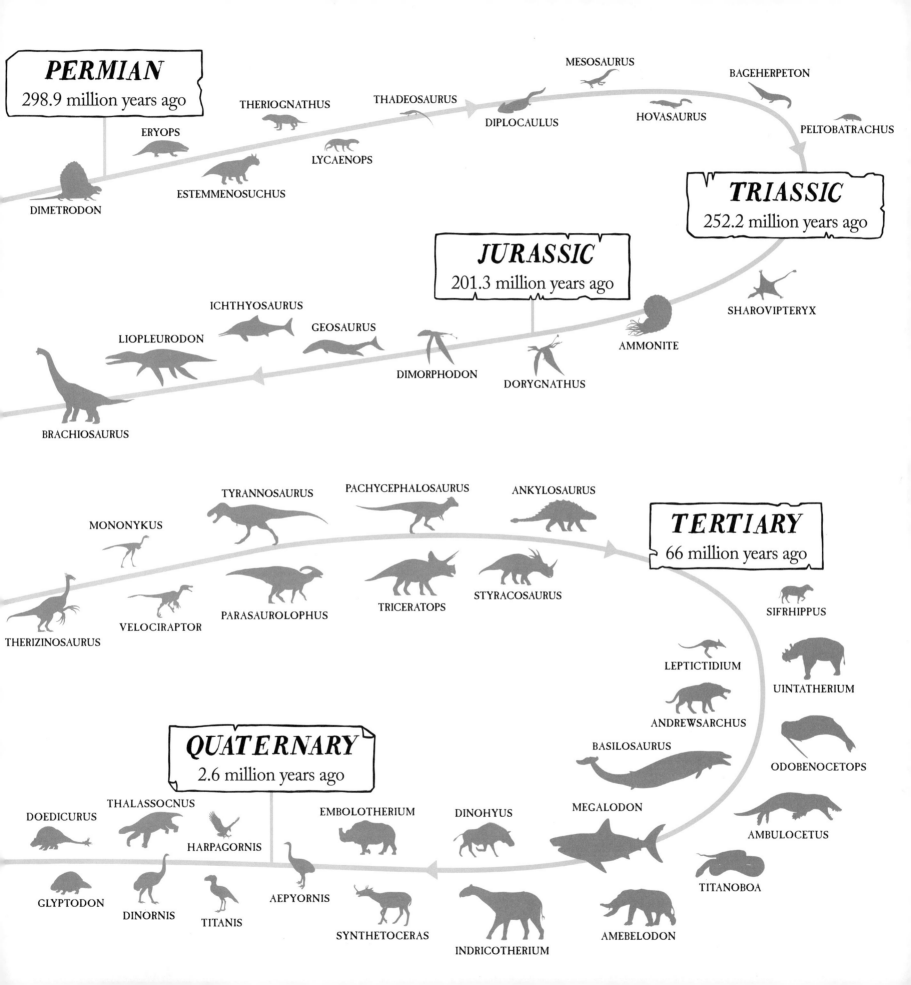

PERMIAN
298.9 million years ago

THERIOGNATHUS

ERYOPS

LYCAENOPS

ESTEMMENOSUCHUS

DIMETRODON

THADEOSAURUS

DIPLOCAULUS

MESOSAURUS

HOVASAURUS

BAGEHERPETON

PELTOBATRACHUS

TRIASSIC
252.2 million years ago

JURASSIC
201.3 million years ago

SHAROVIPTERYX

ICHTHYOSAURUS

GEOSAURUS

LIOPLEURODON

DIMORPHODON

DORYGNATHUS

AMMONITE

BRACHIOSAURUS

TYRANNOSAURUS

PACHYCEPHALOSAURUS

ANKYLOSAURUS

MONONYKUS

TERTIARY
66 million years ago

VELOCIRAPTOR

PARASAUROLOPHUS

TRICERATOPS

STYRACOSAURUS

THERIZINOSAURUS

SIFRHIPPUS

LEPTICTIDIUM

UINTATHERIUM

ANDREWSARCHUS

ODOBENOCETOPS

BASILOSAURUS

QUATERNARY
2.6 million years ago

THALASSOCNUS

EMBOLOTHERIUM

DINOHYUS

MEGALODON

AMBULOCETUS

DOEDICURUS

HARPAGORNIS

GLYPTODON

DINORNIS

TITANIS

AEPYORNIS

SYNTHETOCERAS

INDRICOTHERIUM

AMEBELODON

TITANOBOA

INTRODUCTION

The incredible creatures in this book have been compiled and categorized into four chapters, each focusing on different periods:

- *DEVONIAN, CARBONIFEROUS & PERMIAN*
- *TRIASSIC & JURASSIC*
- *CRETACEOUS*
- *TERTIARY & QUATERNARY*

Color in each striking illustration—then turn the page to find out all about the ferocious and fascinating creatures that once roamed the prehistoric wilderness.

First edition for the United States and Canada published in 2018
by Barron's Educational Series, Inc.

First published in Great Britain in 2017 by Buster Books, an imprint of Michael O'Mara
Books Limited, 9 Lion Yard, Tremadoc Road, London SW4 7NQ

All inquiries should be addressed to:
Barron's Educational Series, Inc.
250 Wireless Boulevard
Hauppauge, NY 11788
www.barronseduc.com

ISBN: 978-1-4380-1160-8

Date of Manufacture: May 2018
Manufactured by: W06K06T, Tsuen Wan, Hong Kong, China

Printed in China
9 8 7 6 5 4 3 2 1

DEVONIAN, CARBONIFEROUS & PERMIAN

DUNKLEOSTEUS

DEVONIAN, CARBONIFEROUS & PERMIAN

419.2 million years ago – 358.9 million years ago – 298.9 million years ago – 252.2 million years ago

During the Devonian Period (sometimes known as the "Age of Fishes"), a huge variety of creatures that lived in and beside water appeared. These included the first bony fish and sharklike creatures with skeletons made from a substance called cartilage. The first forests sprouted from the soil, and huge trees erupted into the air.

This spell of great growth and expansion continued into the Carboniferous Period. Oxygen levels in the atmosphere soared to the highest the planet has ever known, and forests and swamps dominated the landscape. It was at this time that the majority of Earth's coal (fossilized carbon) began to form from all the lush vegetation.

The Permian Period, however, was a tougher time. At the end of the Carboniferous Period, the planet became locked in an ice age, but temperatures soared during the Permian Period. Dense forests and fertile swamps became dry deserts and wastelands. Animals struggled to live in these harsh landscapes, and approximately 95 percent of all sea life and 70 percent of land species died out during this time. This marked the most devastating extinction planet Earth has ever known.

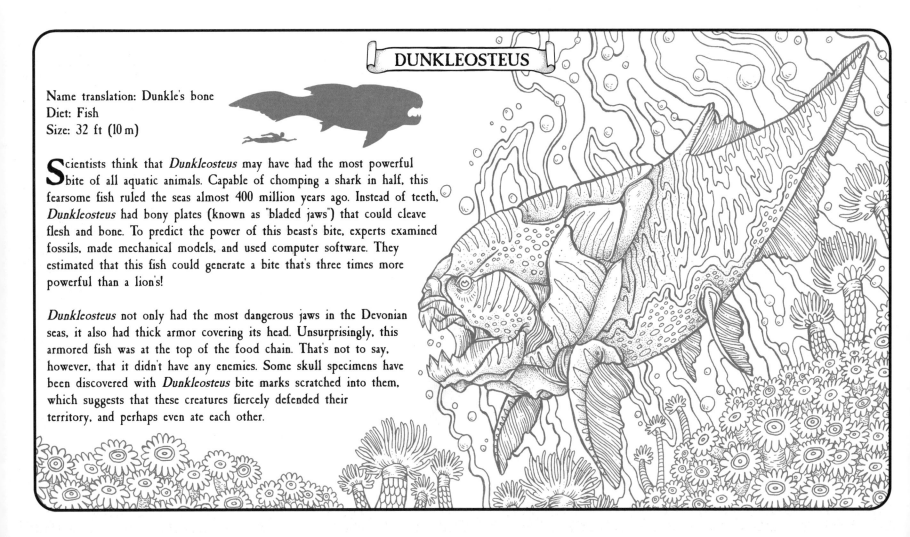

DUNKLEOSTEUS

Name translation: Dunkle's bone
Diet: Fish
Size: 32 ft (10 m)

Scientists think that *Dunkleosteus* may have had the most powerful bite of all aquatic animals. Capable of chomping a shark in half, this fearsome fish ruled the seas almost 400 million years ago. Instead of teeth, *Dunkleosteus* had bony plates (known as "bladed jaws") that could cleave flesh and bone. To predict the power of this beast's bite, experts examined fossils, made mechanical models, and used computer software. They estimated that this fish could generate a bite that's three times more powerful than a lion's!

Dunkleosteus not only had the most dangerous jaws in the Devonian seas, it also had thick armor covering its head. Unsurprisingly, this armored fish was at the top of the food chain. That's not to say, however, that it didn't have any enemies. Some skull specimens have been discovered with *Dunkleosteus* bite marks scratched into them, which suggests that these creatures fiercely defended their territory, and perhaps even ate each other.

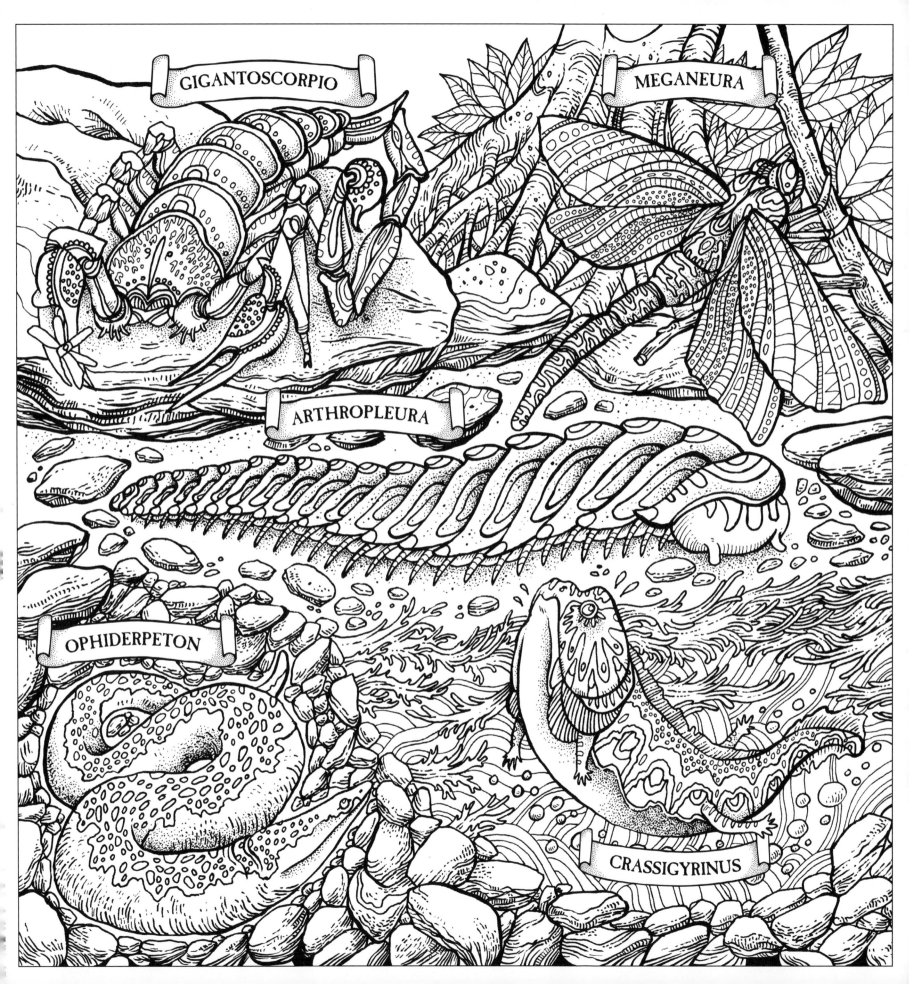

GIGANTOSCORPIO

Name translation: Giant scorpion
Diet: Insects and small reptiles
Size: 35 in (90 cm)

Gigantoscorpio was as large as a domestic cat, and some experts believe that its sheer size suggests it may well have lived in or close to water (like modern-day crabs).

Regardless of their size, all known scorpion species alive today are venomous, and it's likely that *Gigantoscorpio* was, too.

MEGANEURA

Name translation: Large-nerved
Diet: Insects and small amphibians
Size: 27 in (70 cm) wingspan

Meganeura is the largest winged insect ever discovered. Despite its vast size, *Meganeura* probably looked very similar to a modern-day dragonfly.

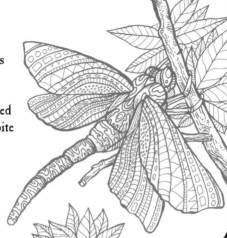

ARTHROPLEURA

Name translation: Jointed ribs
Diet: Plants
Size: 7.5 ft (2.3 m)

The existence of *Arthropleura* shows how the oxygen-rich atmosphere during the Carboniferous Period allowed animals to grow on a stupendously grand scale. It could measure up to 20 inches (50 centimeters) wide and grow to be bigger than a human being.

This millipede-like animal had a tough exoskeleton (armored casing) and is the largest arthropod (an invertebrate animal with a segmented body and jointed limbs) ever discovered.

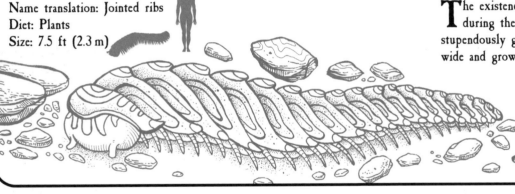

OPHIDERPETON

Name translation: Snake amphibian
Diet: Small insects and invertebrates
Size: 31 in (80 cm)

This snake-like creature had more than 200 vertebrae (spinal bones) in its body. It lived in wetlands and swamps where it burrowed and hunted.

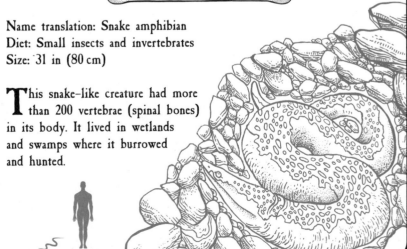

CRASSIGYRINUS

Name translation: Thick frog
Diet: Fish
Size: 6 ft (2 m)

With a pair of long fangs and a mouth full of sharp teeth, *Crassigyrinus* was a fierce predator. Its tiny limbs suggest that its ancestors may have once lived beside water, rather than in it.

DIMETRODON

Name translation: Two measures of teeth
Diet: Amphibians and reptiles
Size: 11.5 ft (3.5 m)

Roughly 50 million years before the first dinosaurs appeared, the prehistoric reptile known as *Dimetrodon* ruled the wilderness. Current evidence from the structure of its bones suggests that *Dimetrodon* was cold blooded and would have relied on its surroundings to warm or cool its body. It probably used its huge sail to help regulate its temperature. It could bask in sunlight to warm up, or tilt its sail into the wind or shade to cool down. By making *Dimetrodon* look much bigger and more imposing than it actually was, the sail may have also deterred other carnivorous creatures from attacking it.

Early drawings of this reptile portray the beast with a short, stumpy tail (or with no tail at all). This is because a specimen with its tail intact was not uncovered until almost 50 years after *Dimetrodon* was first discovered.

ESTEMMENOSUCHUS

Name translation: Crowned crocodile
Diet: Plants; possibly carrion (decaying animals)
Size: 10 ft (3 m)

Roughly the same size as a rhinoceros, *Estemmenosuchus* had rugged bumps and horns protruding from its head and smooth, hairless skin. Despite its fierce appearance and large canine teeth, this reptile was a plant eater. The teeth at the back of its mouth were much flatter than those at the front, making them perfect for crushing and mashing vegetation.

Experts believe that *Estemmenosuchus* was probably quite an awkward and clumsy animal. Its forelegs sprawled to its sides, and fossil evidence suggests that this animal had only a small number of bones in its feet, which would have limited its movement. It may have walked a bit like a salamander or a platypus.

LYCAENOPS

Name translation: Wolf face
Diet: Small reptiles and mammal-like creatures
Size: 3 ft (1 m)

This creature's canine teeth were used for chomping, biting, and piercing its prey. It probably hunted like a Komodo dragon (a large lizard you can see today)—using its jagged teeth to strip large chunks of flesh from prey, then gulping the meat down whole.

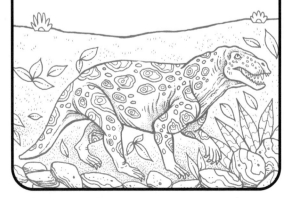

MICROBRACHIS

Name translation: Small arm
Diet: Insects and other small invertebrates
Size: 6 in (15 cm)

Unlike most amphibians that have gills inside their bodies, this tiny creature had external gills that permanently protruded from its neck.

Microbrachis probably looked very similar to a Mexican creature called an axolotl. Axolotls exist in the world today, but they are quite rare.

THERIOGNATHUS

Name translation: Mammal jaw
Diet: Small reptiles
Size: 4 ft (1.2 m)

This rodent-like reptile had many of the same features as mammals, most notably a furry coat. Beneath all its fur, however, *Theriognathus* would have looked similar to *Lycaenops*.

THADEOSAURUS

Name translation: Thadeo's lizard
Diet: Small fish, invertebrates, and freshwater creatures
Size: 24 in (60 cm)

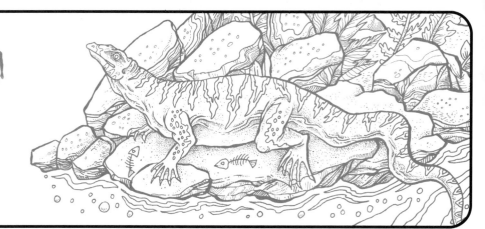

Thadeosaurus had an extraordinarily long tail that it wiggled and waved to propel itself through the water. Its chest muscles and leg muscles were well developed, which suggests that this reptile was also a talented sprinter and, perhaps, an agile climber, too.

HOVASAURUS

Name translation: Hova lizard
Diet: Small fish, invertebrates, and freshwater creatures
Size: 20 in (50 cm)

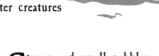

Stones and small pebbles were found in the belly of a fossilized *Hovasaurus*, suggesting that it used the gravel as ballast (weight) to maintain its stability when diving. Divers sometimes strap weights to their belts for the same purpose.

Hovasaurus, like the rest of the creatures on this page, lived in freshwater lakes, rivers, and ponds. *Hovasaurus* was well suited to a life in the water, with a strong, muscular tail and heavily webbed feet.

MESOSAURUS

Name translation: Middle lizard
Diet: Tiny invertebrates
Size: 18 in (45 cm)

Mesosaurus had lots of fine teeth that it used to filter food and webbed feet to improve its efficiency when wading through water.

Fossilized remains of this creature have been found in both South America and South Africa. As a result of this, scientists reconstruct these continents as once being part of the same ancient landmass. *Mesosaurus* didn't live in salt water, so it definitely couldn't have swum across the sea. The merging and breaking apart of continents is due to a process called "plate tectonics."

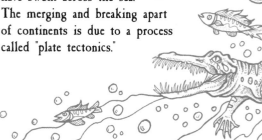

DIPLOCAULUS

Name translation: Double caul
Diet: Fish
Size: 3 ft (1 m)

This animal's most prominent characteristic was its banana- or boomerang-shaped head, which scientists believe may have helped the creature power through water, or perhaps prevented it from being swept away by strong currents. Its large head could also have deterred other animals from attacking it or eating it.

ERYOPS

Name translation: Drawn-out face
Diet: Fish
Size: 7 ft (2 m)

Eryops lived along river banks, swamps, and lakes. It didn't have the ability to chew, so it had to lift its head to force food to the back of its throat (in the same way that crocodiles and alligators eat). Because it was well suited to life on land and in water, this animal thrived during the Permian Period.

PELTOBATRACHUS

Name translation: Armored amphibian
Diet: Insects
Size: 28 in (70 cm)

Like an armadillo, *Peltobatrachus* was covered (from neck to tail) in strong plates of armor. Its protective layer was much more robust than the armor of other creatures, and its bones were thick and heavy-set, especially in its skull. As a result, *Peltobatrachus* was well adapted to fend off attacks from the large fearsome predators of its time.

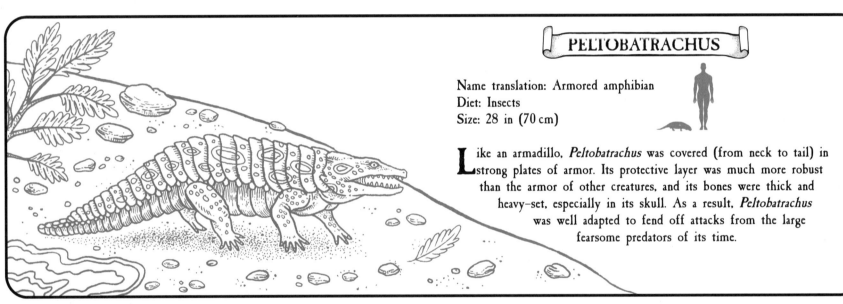

BAGEHERPETON

Name translation: Crawling animal from Bagé city
Diet: Fish and small river-dwelling creatures
Size: 7 ft (2 m)

Found in the region of Rio Grande do Sul in Brazil, *Bageherpeton* was probably similar in appearance to a crocodile, with its long jaw and conical (cone-shaped) teeth. It may have behaved like a modern-day gharial (a fish-catching species of crocodile native to north Indian rivers). The bones in this animal's lower jaw were extremely strong and dense, suggesting that it could bite with immense speed and strength.

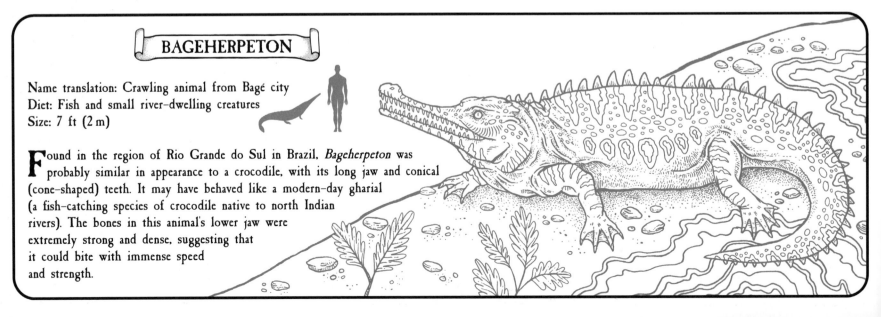

TRIASSIC & JURASSIC

BRACHIOSAURUS

LUSOTITAN

TRIASSIC & JURASSIC

252.2 million years ago – 201.3 million years ago – 145 million years ago

At the beginning of the Triassic Period, all of Earth's land was squashed together, forming one gigantic supercontinent known as Pangaea. The majority of this vast area was dry and barren. Deserts and wastelands dominated the landscape, and the planet couldn't sustain or support a variety of organisms. Part way through the Triassic Period, however, the land began to divide and split, forming two separate continents. This created new coastlines, giving more and more animals and plants access to water, spawning new species of flora and fauna. The air grew more humid and rich in moisture. However, it wasn't until the Mid-to-Late Triassic Period that dinosaurs really began to flourish.

The Jurassic Period marked a new dawn for the age of dinosaurs. Rainforests began to sprout and areas inland became sustainable. Carnivorous dinosaurs grew bigger and stronger by feasting on a wealth of plant-eating animals. Pterosaurs and early species of birds took to the skies, and the sea was stocked with plenty of fish and marine monsters. A wonderful variety of animals existed, sparking what some scientists call the "golden age" of dinosaurs.

BRACHIOSAURUS

Name translation: Arm lizard
Diet: Leaves
Size: 72 ft (22 m)

An animal of this size and stature must have had a huge appetite. In fact, it is estimated that *Brachiosaurus* ate somewhere between 450 and 900 pounds (200 and 400 kilograms) of plant matter per day.

The microscopic structure of the bones of *Brachiosaurus* and other dinosaurs is very similar to that of mammals and birds. Because of this, scientists believe that dinosaur bones grew quickly. Fast growth requires a fast metabolism, leading scientists to conclude that most dinosaurs were warm-blooded. *Brachiosaurus'* bones and guts were full of large air sacs that would have helped to prevent it from overheating in the hot Jurassic climate.

LUSOTITAN

Name translation: Giant from Portugal
Diet: Leaves
Size: 82 ft (25 m)

The first *Lusotitan* fossils were found in 1947 in Portugal. This dinosaur, like *Brachiosaurus*, had long front legs and an extremely long neck so that it could feast on the foliage at the tops of tall trees. In this way, it had access to food that other animals simply couldn't reach.

GEOSAURUS

Name translation: Earth lizard
Diet: Fish
Size: 10 ft (3 m)

Geosaurus belonged to the crocodile family and was an extremely gifted fish-catcher. Its thin, streamlined frame could cut swiftly through water, and its powerful muscular tail could propel it forward with speed and ferocity. When scientists first discovered *Geosaurus* remains, they assumed that it lived on land, hence its name ("geo" means "earth" in ancient Greek). This beast also had a special gland that removed excess salt from the water it drank.

ICHTHYOSAURUS

Name translation: Fish lizard
Diet: Fish
Size: 7 ft (2 m)

Ichthyosaurus relied heavily on its eyesight to spot and catch prey. Its eyeballs were extremely large and incredibly efficient in areas of low light. In fact, compared to its body size, *Ichthyosaurus* had some of the biggest eyes in the animal kingdom. *Ichthyosaurus* didn't completely rely on its eyes, however, as it also used its ears to hunt. Its eardrums were made of bone and could sense small vibrations in the water.

AMMONITE

Name translation: Rock of Ammon
Diet: Plankton, small crustaceans, and possibly larger prey
Size: Ranging from a couple of inches in diameter to
    8 ft (2.5 m) across

Ammonite shells consisted of several individual chambers. As the creature aged, it added more chambers to its shell. Because of this, experts can guess how old an ammonite was, based on its size.

Different species of ammonite were different shapes and probably had different diets. Bulbous ones may have drifted and filtered plankton. Narrow ones were probably swift hunters, and heavy, lumpy ones foraged on the seafloor.

LIOPLEURODON

Name translation: Smooth-sided tooth
Diet: Sea-dwelling creatures
Size: 20 ft (6 m)

One of the most ferocious animals to inhabit prehistoric seas, *Liopleurodon* ruled the waves during the Late Jurassic Period. Scientists believe that it had a strong sense of smell and was able to sniff out prey in the dark depths of the ocean.

Very few bones from the body have ever been discovered. Although large skulls (about 3 feet (1 meter) in length) and long teeth (almost twice as long as the fangs of a *Tyrannosaurus*) have been found in good condition. *Liopleurodon* had a typical pliosaur limb arrangement, with four flippers that provided excellent acceleration in water.

Liopleurodon, like whales, couldn't breathe under water because they didn't have gills. It is predicted, though, that they could hold their breath for up to one hour and dive to great depths to catch prey.

ALLOSAURUS

STEGOSAURUS

ALLOSAURUS

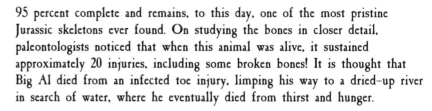

Name translation: Different lizard
Diet: Plant-eating dinosaurs
    (small stegosaurs, for instance)
Size: 39 ft (12 m)

In 1991, fossil hunters made an incredible discovery when they unearthed an almost-entirely-intact skeleton of a teenage *Allosaurus* in an ancient riverbed. Nicknamed "Big Al," the specimen (found in Wyoming) was 95 percent complete and remains, to this day, one of the most pristine Jurassic skeletons ever found. On studying the bones in closer detail, paleontologists noticed that when this animal was alive, it sustained approximately 20 injuries, including some broken bones! It is thought that Big Al died from an infected toe injury, limping his way to a dried-up river in search of water, where he eventually died from thirst and hunger.

Paleontologists can learn a great deal from inspecting dinosaur remains. Experts noticed, for instance, that some *Allosaurus* skeletons had puncture wounds, most likely caused by the sharp spikes on stegosaur tails, and some stegosaurs had marks and indentations matching the bite of an *Allosaurus*. As a result of this, paleontologists are fairly certain that theropods (the group of dinosaurs to which *Allosaurus* belongs) fought or even ate stegosaurs.

STEGOSAURUS

Name translation: Roof lizard
Diet: Low-lying plants
Size: 30 ft (9 m)

One of the most recognizable dinosaurs, *Stegosaurus* had two rows of plates running along its backbone. Whether these plates were for temperature regulation, defense, or just for show, is still a mystery. Some experts now think that the plates played an important part in attracting a mate.

Stegosaurus could grow to be the size of a van and weigh almost 6,600 pounds (3,000 kilograms). Although their size alone was probably enough to ward off most hunters, the beast's spiked tail was, by far, its most effective defense. The spines could grow to almost 35 inches (90 centimeters) in length. Stegosaurs could thrash their colossal tails, striking the spikes against enemies to inflict piercing injuries. The *Stegosaurus* shown in this illustration is just a baby, so not as fierce or powerful as a full-grown adult.

In relation to its size, *Stegosaurus* had a smaller brain (measuring roughly the same size as a lime) than any other dinosaur.

DIMORPHODON

Name translation: Two types of teeth
Diet: Insects and fish
Size: 4.6 ft (1.4 m) wingspan

To improve its ability in the air, this pterosaur (flying lizard) had flimsy, lightweight bones and hollow cavities in its skull to keep its weight to an absolute minimum. *Dimorphodon* also had strong legs and claws so that it could clamber up cliffs.

DORYGNATHUS

Name translation: Spear jaw
Diet: Fish
Size: 3 ft (1 m) wingspan

Dorygnathus, a talented fish-catcher, had protruding teeth at the front of its lower jaw—perfect for snatching at prey. In much the same way that a plant called the Venus fly trap functions, when this animal's jaws were closed its teeth interlocked, forming an almost inescapable trap.

GNATHOSAURUS

Name translation: Jaw lizard
Diet: Invertebrates and fish
Size: 5.6 ft (1.7 m) wingspan

When it was first discovered, paleontologists thought that *Gnathosaurus* was some sort of crocodile. Its jaws, lined with 130 needle-like teeth, bore a strong resemblance to those of crocodiles and alligators.

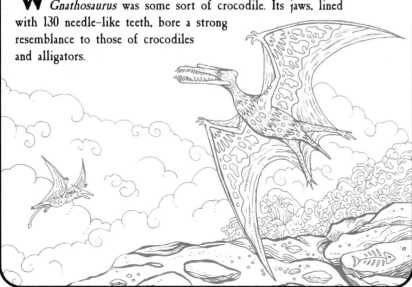

PTERODACTYLUS

Name translation: Wing finger
Diet: Fish
Size: 8 ft (2.5 m) wingspan

Pterodactylus is a perfect example of how difficult it can be to identify and categorize an animal that existed more than 150 million years ago. Experts originally thought this creature was a bat-like mammal, then a swimming animal (that used its wings like giant paddles), before eventually settling on the flying pterosaur that we are now familiar with.

ARCHAEOPTERYX

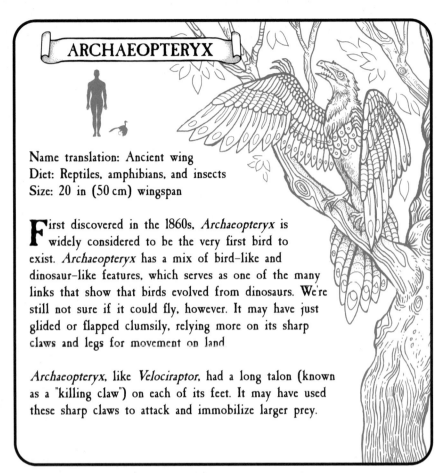

Name translation: Ancient wing
Diet: Reptiles, amphibians, and insects
Size: 20 in (50 cm) wingspan

First discovered in the 1860s, *Archaeopteryx* is widely considered to be the very first bird to exist. *Archaeopteryx* has a mix of bird-like and dinosaur-like features, which serves as one of the many links that show that birds evolved from dinosaurs. We're still not sure if it could fly, however. It may have just glided or flapped clumsily, relying more on its sharp claws and legs for movement on land.

Archaeopteryx, like *Velociraptor*, had a long talon (known as a "killing claw") on each of its feet. It may have used these sharp claws to attack and immobilize larger prey.

SHAROVIPTERYX

Name translation: Sharov's wing
Diet: Insects
Size: 12 in (30 cm)

Sharovipteryx was a reptile, not a bird, and would glide rather than fly. This beast was extremely unusual in that its back legs (rather than its forelegs) had a large flap of skin, which it could pull taut and use to float through the air.

A similar principle can be seen today in the way flying squirrels glide from tree to tree, and in skydivers' wing suits.

MICRORAPTOR

Name translation: Small thief or hunter
Diet: Small insects, mammals, and fish
Size: 20 in (50 cm) wingspan

Microraptor had four feathered wings, rather than two, which it used to glide. Each wing was covered in dense plumage, giving the creature a large surface area, allowing it to soar through the air more efficiently.

CAUDIPTERYX

Name translation: Feathered tail
Diet: Small insects, mammals, and fish
Size: 31 in (80 cm) wingspan

Roughly the size of a small peacock, *Caudipteryx* was incapable of flying or even gliding. The long feathers protruding from its arms and tail were most likely for display.

DIPLODOCUS

CERATOSAURUS

DIPLODOCUS

Name translation: Double beam
Diet: Plants
Size: 112 ft (34 m)

Diplodocus wins the award for the longest dinosaur, thanks to its incredibly long neck and whip-like tail. Its estimated size makes it longer than the blue whale (the biggest animal ever to exist on Earth), but not quite as heavy or bulky.

Some scientists believe that *Diplodocus* was capable of springing up onto its hind legs to reach even the tallest trees and highest branches.

CERATOSAURUS

Name translation: Horned lizard
Diet: Plant-eating dinosaurs
Size: 20 ft (6 m)

Ceratosaurus had large knife-like teeth, spiky horns above its eyes, and a longer horn on top of its nose. It had a terrifying appearance and may well have hunted in packs. Some scientists suspect that *Ceratosaurus* was a strong swimmer. It may have spent a great deal of its time in rivers, using its tail to propel it forward in much the same way that iguanas swim today.

This dinosaur was first discovered by an American paleontologist named Othniel Charles Marsh. He was a pioneer in his field and one of the most famous paleontologists of the time, helping to discover more than 1,000 fossils. Marsh had a fierce rivalry with a man named Edward Drinker Cope, and each wanted to discover more species and bigger fossils than the other. This bitter competition became known as the Bone Wars.

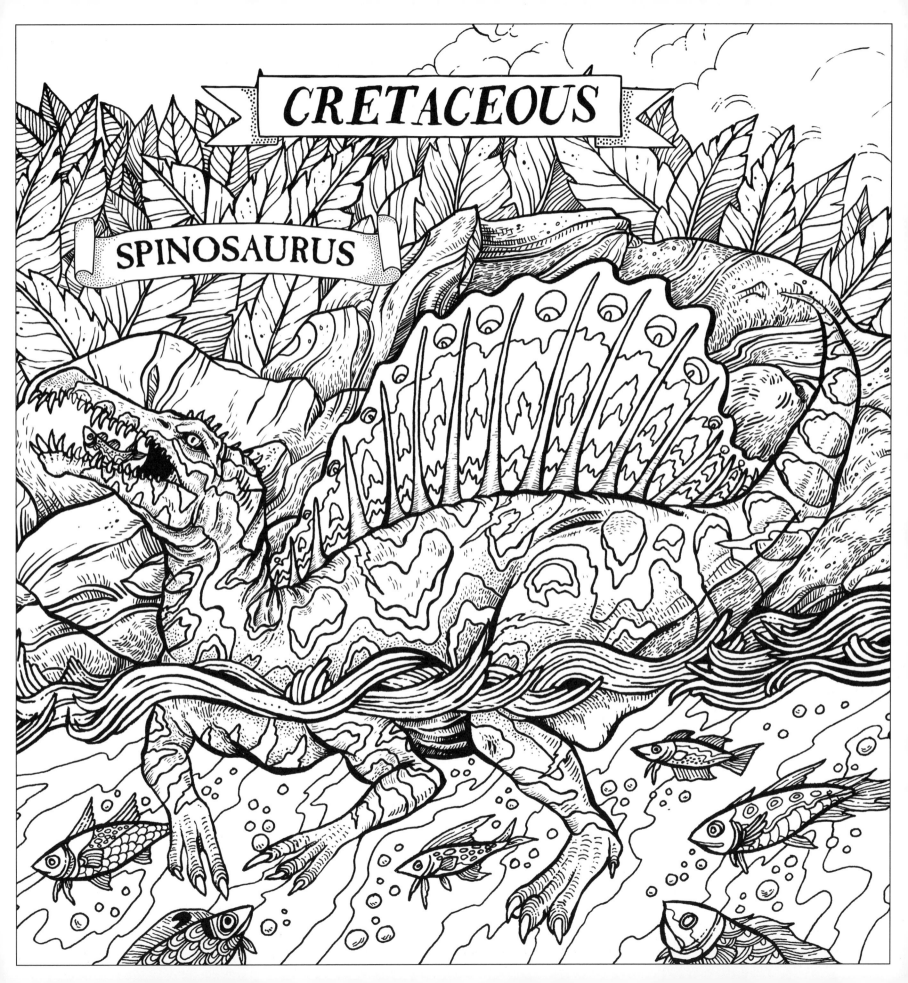

CRETACEOUS

SPINOSAURUS

CRETACEOUS

145 million years ago – 66 million years ago

For many paleontologists and scientists, the Cretaceous Period produced the most exciting and varied animals. Never before, or since, have the planet's animals been, collectively, so colossal. Giant carnivores roamed the terrain, terrific pterosaurs soared in the skies, and gargantuan monsters skulked in the dark depths of the seas. This high point in the reign of dinosaurs also marked the moment in time where the first modern insect, mammal, and bird groups, and the first flowering plants, flourished. This paved the way for new types of animals to thrive after the dinosaurs died out.

The Cretaceous Period was extremely warm. Temperatures soared and sea levels rose as the ice caps at the poles melted. Across the globe, volcanoes spewed lava and released toxic gases into the atmosphere. These gases caused temperatures to rise even higher, producing a greenhouse effect.

This era ended with the extinction of the dinosaurs. It is widely acknowledged that an enormous meteorite, measuring about 6 miles (10 kilometers) wide, struck Earth near the Yucatan Peninsula in Mexico. On impact, this meteorite created a crater more than 110 miles (180 kilometers) wide, kicking plumes of dust into the air and sending violent tremors across the earth. The dust would have blotted out the sun, causing plants and animals to die in darkness. Although the meteorite was perhaps not the sole reason for such a mass extinction, it played a huge part in bringing the dinosaur dynasty to an abrupt end.

SPINOSAURUS

Name translation: Spined lizard
Diet: Fish and river-dwelling creatures
Size: 56 ft (17 m)

The first *Spinosaurus* remains ever discovered (in Egypt, in 1912) were destroyed by bombing raids during World War II. Since then, there have been few *Spinosaurus* fossils (other than tiny bone fragments) in circulation, and for more than a century, very little was known about this dinosaur. In 2014, however, paleontologists unearthed a giant specimen in the Sahara Desert, and the scientific findings that followed have been staggering.

Spinosaurus is the largest carnivorous dinosaur ever discovered. It lived predominantly on a diet of fish and other marine creatures, and probably dwelt near rivers and other bodies of water. Its head was similar in shape to that of a crocodile, and its long, cone-shaped teeth were perfect for snapping up aquatic animals. By looking closely at the shape of its wide feet and at its bone density, paleontologists think *Spinosaurus* was a keen swimmer, too. Experts believe that it lived both on land

and in water, like crocodiles and alligators. The sail on the beast's back is still a mystery. At a height of almost 7 feet (2 meters), it formed a colossal wall that may have helped regulate the dinosaur's body temperature, although it may have also been used to attract a mate or to ward off any other predatory dinosaurs.

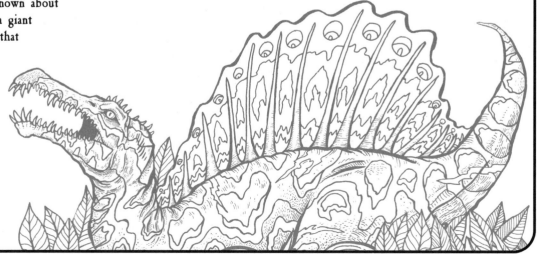

QUETZALCOATLUS

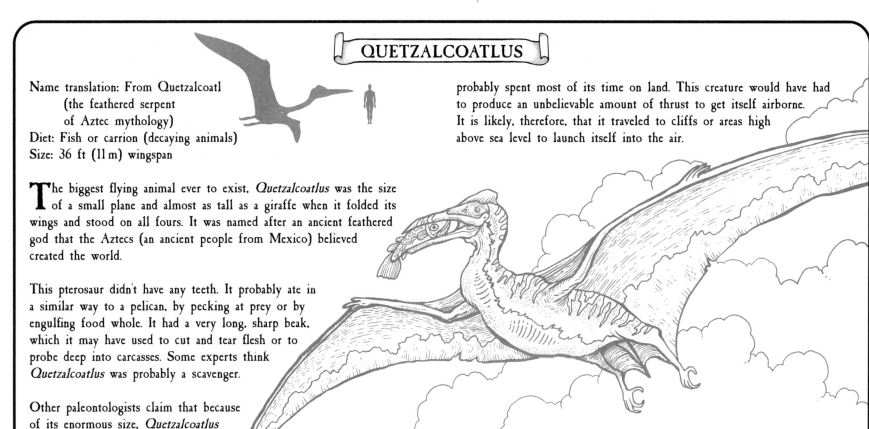

Name translation: From Quetzalcoatl
    (the feathered serpent
    of Aztec mythology)
Diet: Fish or carrion (decaying animals)
Size: 36 ft (11 m) wingspan

The biggest flying animal ever to exist, *Quetzalcoatlus* was the size of a small plane and almost as tall as a giraffe when it folded its wings and stood on all fours. It was named after an ancient feathered god that the Aztecs (an ancient people from Mexico) believed created the world.

This pterosaur didn't have any teeth. It probably ate in a similar way to a pelican, by pecking at prey or by engulfing food whole. It had a very long, sharp beak, which it may have used to cut and tear flesh or to probe deep into carcasses. Some experts think *Quetzalcoatlus* was probably a scavenger.

Other paleontologists claim that because of its enormous size, *Quetzalcoatlus*

probably spent most of its time on land. This creature would have had to produce an unbelievable amount of thrust to get itself airborne. It is likely, therefore, that it traveled to cliffs or areas high above sea level to launch itself into the air.

PTERANODON

Name translation: Wing without teeth
Diet: Fish
Size: 30 ft (9 m) wingspan

Pteranodon, like most pterosaurs, had hollow bones to keep its weight down, making it easier to fly. Its cranium was enormous; in fact, its head (including the crest and beak) was even bigger than its body.

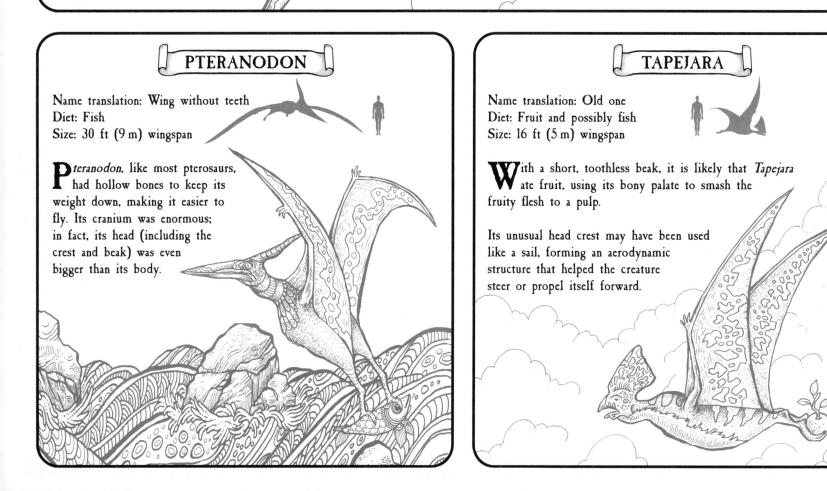

TAPEJARA

Name translation: Old one
Diet: Fruit and possibly fish
Size: 16 ft (5 m) wingspan

With a short, toothless beak, it is likely that *Tapejara* ate fruit, using its bony palate to smash the fruity flesh to a pulp.

Its unusual head crest may have been used like a sail, forming an aerodynamic structure that helped the creature steer or propel itself forward.

IGUANODON

Name translation: Iguana tooth
Diet: Plants, seeds, and leaves
Size: 33 ft (10 m)

Iguanodon, unlike most dinosaurs, was equally capable of walking on all fours or on its hind legs. This would have been extremely useful when the creature was grazing on low-lying plants or when it was stretching to grasp vegetation in trees. To make grazing even easier, *Iguanodon* also had nimble fingers and a pointed spike on its thumbs, which it may have used to break into seeds, to strip leaves from branches, or to defend itself against predators.

Scientists are fairly certain that *Iguanodon* lived in herds. This breakthrough came in 1878, when more than 30 *Iguanodon* skeletons were discovered together in a coal mine in Belgium.

UTAHRAPTOR

Name translation: Thief or hunter from Utah
Diet: Plant-eating dinosaurs
Size: 20 ft (6 m)

Utahraptor had a "killing claw" on each hind foot that was 9 inches (24 centimeters) long, which it used to slash at prey, inflicting deep wounds and injuries.

Utahraptor had very thick bones in its legs, suggesting that it was very powerful, but perhaps not as fast as other raptors or dinosaurs. It is likely, therefore, that this predator ambushed and attacked prey, and then stalked its target until it collapsed from fatigue or blood loss.

HYPSILOPHODON

Name translation: *Hypsilurus* tooth
Diet: Plants
Size: 7.5 ft (2.3 m)

Hypsilophodon had special protruding bones in its skull that helped protect its eyes from strong sunlight. To date, fossilized *Hypsilophodon* bones have only been found on a tiny island (Isle of Wight) off the south coast of England.

ELASMOSAURUS

TYLOSAURUS

ELASMOSAURUS

Name translation: Metal-plate lizard
Diet: Fish
Size: 39 ft (12 m)

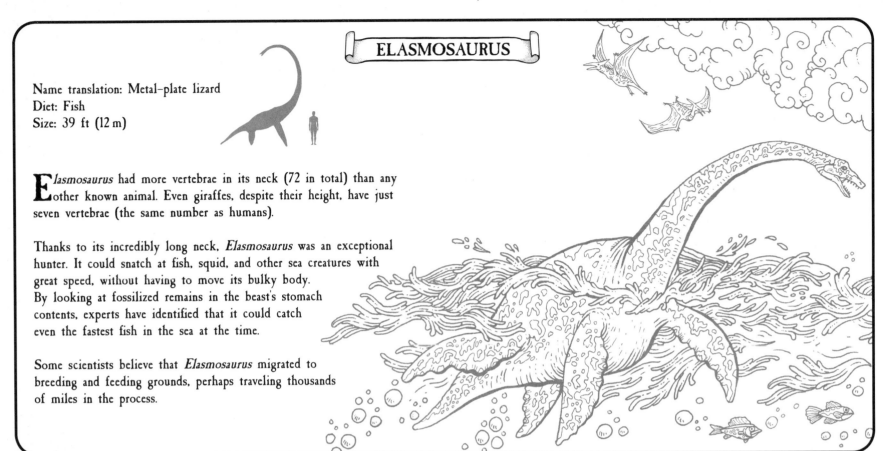

Elasmosaurus had more vertebrae in its neck (72 in total) than any other known animal. Even giraffes, despite their height, have just seven vertebrae (the same number as humans).

Thanks to its incredibly long neck, *Elasmosaurus* was an exceptional hunter. It could snatch at fish, squid, and other sea creatures with great speed, without having to move its bulky body. By looking at fossilized remains in the beast's stomach contents, experts have identified that it could catch even the fastest fish in the sea at the time.

Some scientists believe that *Elasmosaurus* migrated to breeding and feeding grounds, perhaps traveling thousands of miles in the process.

TYLOSAURUS

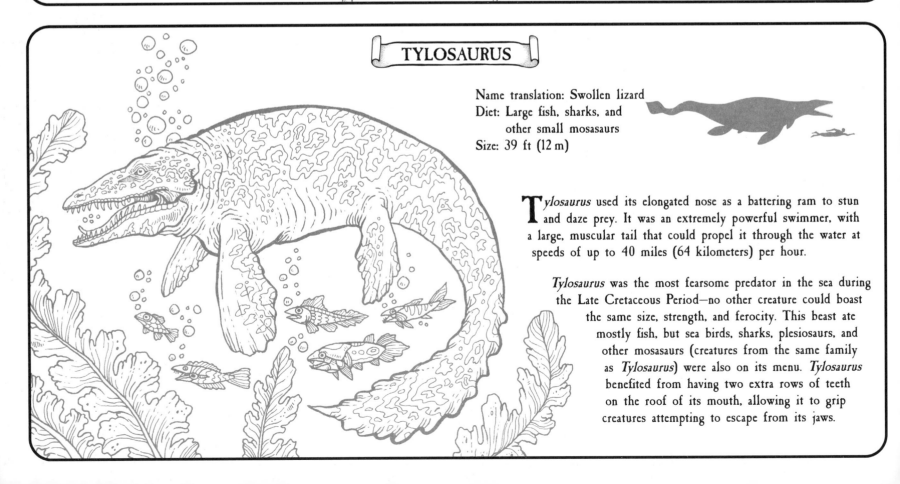

Name translation: Swollen lizard
Diet: Large fish, sharks, and
   other small mosasaurs
Size: 39 ft (12 m)

Tylosaurus used its elongated nose as a battering ram to stun and daze prey. It was an extremely powerful swimmer, with a large, muscular tail that could propel it through the water at speeds of up to 40 miles (64 kilometers) per hour.

Tylosaurus was the most fearsome predator in the sea during the Late Cretaceous Period—no other creature could boast the same size, strength, and ferocity. This beast ate mostly fish, but sea birds, sharks, plesiosaurs, and other mosasaurs (creatures from the same family as *Tylosaurus*) were also on its menu. *Tylosaurus* benefited from having two extra rows of teeth on the roof of its mouth, allowing it to grip creatures attempting to escape from its jaws.

NOMINGIA

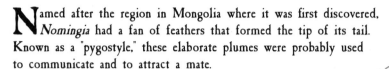

Name translation: From the Nomingiin Gobi
Diet: Probably omnivorous
Size: 5.9 ft (1.8 m)

Named after the region in Mongolia where it was first discovered, *Nomingia* had a fan of feathers that formed the tip of its tail. Known as a "pygostyle," these elaborate plumes were probably used to communicate and to attract a mate.

STRUTHIOMIMUS

Name translation: Ostrich mimic
Diet: Plants
Size: 13 ft (4 m)

With a long neck, small head, long legs, and a short beak, it's no surprise that this animal's name literally means "ostrich mimic."

Known as a "biped," meaning that it walked on its two hind feet, *Struthiomimus* could probably run at speeds of up to 30 miles (50 kilometers) per hour. Today's ostriches, on the other hand, can sprint up to 45 miles (70 kilometers) per hour.

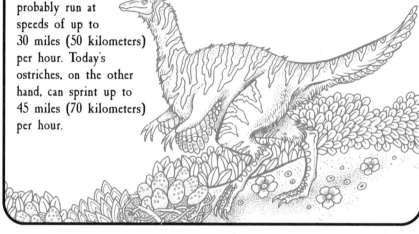

MONONYKUS

Name translation: Single claw
Diet: Insects
Size: 3 ft (1 m)

Mononykus, with its extremely strong but incredibly small arms, has baffled scientists for decades. Many dinosaur experts now think that *Mononykus* used its claws (one at the end of each arm) to hook or fish small insects (ants and termites, for example) out of burrows.

This creature's long, slender legs were well suited to high-speed running, and it is thought that *Mononykus* was probably an extremely agile beast, able to chase after scurrying insects or flee from predators with confidence.

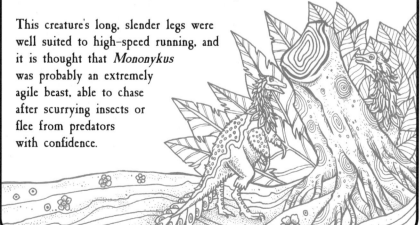

VELOCIRAPTOR

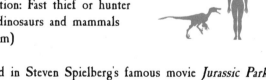

Name translation: Fast thief or hunter
Diet: Small dinosaurs and mammals
Size: 7 ft (2 m)

Immortalized in Steven Spielberg's famous movie *Jurassic Park*, *Velociraptor* was a small, nimble predator with a sharp, sickle-shaped claw on each foot. Unlike Spielberg's representation, however, it is now commonly acknowledged that *Velociraptor* was not lizard-skinned, but was in fact covered in a layer of feathers. *Velociraptor* also wasn't the enormous, muscular creature that it is so often portrayed as in film and television. In reality, a fully-grown adult probably weighed little more than 30 pounds (14 kilograms).

GIGANOTOSAURUS

TYRANNOSAURUS

GIGANOTOSAURUS

Name translation: Giant southern lizard
Diet: Large plant-eating dinosaurs
Size: 49 ft (15 m)

Discovered by amateur fossil-hunter Reuben Carolini in Patagonia (an area of Argentina) in 1993, *Giganotosaurus* could weigh up to 18,000 pounds (8,000 kilograms). Its head alone was larger than a full-grown human being, although its brain was probably no bigger than a banana.

Experts now believe, although the theory is still unproven, that some species of *Giganotosaurus* may have hunted in packs. The remains of at least seven *Mapusaurus* (a close relative of *Giganotosaurus*) specimens were discovered in Argentina in just one site, prompting paleontologists to conclude that they were social animals. This could mean, in theory, that *Giganotosaurus* could hunt even the largest animals of the time.

TYRANNOSAURUS

Name translation: Tyrant lizard
Diet: Carrion (decaying animals) and medium-sized dinosaurs
Size: 39 ft (12 m)

Before the discovery of bigger beasts, such as *Giganotosaurus* and *Spinosaurus*, *Tyrannosaurus* (probably the most famous dinosaur of all time) was considered to be the largest and most ferocious land-dwelling carnivore ever to exist. Its stature, size, and raw power ensured that it stood firmly at the top of the food chain during the Late Cretaceous Period.

Although tyrannosaurs were fierce predators and efficient killers, it is widely believed that they were "opportunistic" hunters, unlikely to sprint after prey over long distances, and much more likely to scavenge. It is possible, for instance, that smaller carnivores gathering around a carcass would scatter if a tyrannosaur approached, leaving the larger dinosaur to eat its free meal in relative peace. That's not to say that

Tyrannosaurus didn't actively hunt, too. A fossil of a healed hadrosaurid bone was discovered in 2013 with the tooth of a *Tyrannosaurus* embedded in it. Some paleontologists believe that this provides overwhelming evidence that tyrannosaurs weren't merely scavengers, and that they were prone to ambushing or attacking at close quarters, too.

THERIZINOSAURUS

THERIZINOSAURUS

Name translation: Scythe lizard
Diet: Unknown, but probably plants
Size: 30 ft (9 m)

Therizinosaurus had the longest claws (and the longest finger bones) of any known animal. Measuring up to 30 inches (70 centimeters) in length, its terrific talons were probably used for self-defense and for clutching at plants and foliage. It may even have used its claws to shear bark from trees or to probe into hollows or nests in search of food.

When its fossilized bones were first discovered, experts thought that *Therizinosaurus* was some sort of giant turtle. They believed that its claws may have formed large flippers that it could use to swim or dig. Although skull remains have never been found for *Therizinosaurus*, experts predict that it probably ate plants based on the diet of its close relatives.

PACHYCEPHALOSAURUS

Name translation: Thick-headed lizard
Diet: Low-lying plants
Size: 26 ft (8 m)

The unmistakeable dome on the top of this dinosaur's head was a whopping 8 inches (20 centimeters) thick. Experts used to think that the creature used its cranium as a battering ram, in the same way that horned sheep sometimes charge at enemies or at each other. Some paleontologists now believe that the dome was also used to attract a mate, much like a peacock's feathers.

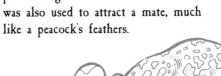

STYRACOSAURUS

Name translation: Spike lizard
Diet: Low-lying plants
Size: 18 ft (5.5 m)

Styracosaurus had a host of horns around the edge of its frill and a huge 2-foot (.5-meter) long spike on its nose.

By looking at fossil evidence, we know that creatures like *Styracosaurus* formed large herds. Known as a "bone bed," thousands of *Styracosaurus* bones (amongst other animal remains) were discovered in an ancient riverbed in Alberta, Canada. Experts think these creatures may all have drowned in the river or possibly died from thirst when the river ran dry.

TRICERATOPS

Name translation: Three-horned face
Diet: Low-lying plants
Size: 30 ft (9 m)

Comparable in size to an African elephant, *Triceratops* could weigh more than a truck and had one of the largest skulls in the animal kingdom. It was a formidable beast for any predator to attack, but it looks as though *Tyrannosaurus* may have actively hunted *Triceratops*. Fossil evidence of the large frill, which was probably used to protect the creature's neck and throat, has been found with holes and tooth marks carved into the bone.

Triceratops had powerful jaws, capable of chomping through dense foliage. Its jowls also housed all of its teeth—*Triceratops* could have as many as 800 teeth embedded in its gums, although it only used 40 or so at a time, replacing each worn-out tooth as it grew older.

TROODON

Name translation: Tearing tooth
Diet: Small nocturnal animals
Size: 7 ft (2 m)

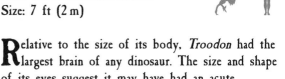

Relative to the size of its body, *Troodon* had the largest brain of any dinosaur. The size and shape of its eyes suggest it may have had an acute sense of sight, prompting scientists to believe it hunted at night.

PARASAUROLOPHUS

Name translation: Near crested lizard
Diet: Plants and leaves
Size: 33 ft (10 m)

For years, the huge crest on top of this dinosaur's head has befuddled scientists. Was it a snorkel-like device used for breathing, a sense-of-smell enhancer, or even a weapon?

Scientists now believe they may know the answer. Evidence suggests that the crest helped these dinosaurs communicate with each other. Paleontologists have made computer models in an attempt to recreate the sound that *Parasaurolophus* would have made. The results have been posted online and can be heard on popular video websites.

ANKYLOSAURUS

Name translation: Fused lizard
Diet: Low-lying plants
Size: 36 ft (11 m)

With a clubbed tail, armor plating, and a heavy-set frame, *Ankylosaurus* was extremely well fortified. If its bulky stature wasn't enough to deter predators, it also had rows of bony spines protruding from its back, neck, and head. Its stocky tail was probably powerful enough to break bones, and the shape of the animal itself—5 feet (1.5 meters) wide with a flattened top—would have been difficult for predators to bite or attack. The only perceived weak spot on a dinosaur of this nature was its unarmored underbelly. *Ankylosaurus* could weigh up to 13,000 pounds (6,000 kilograms), however, so flipping the beast over was no simple task. Despite its somewhat menacing appearance, *Ankylosaurus* was a plant eater.

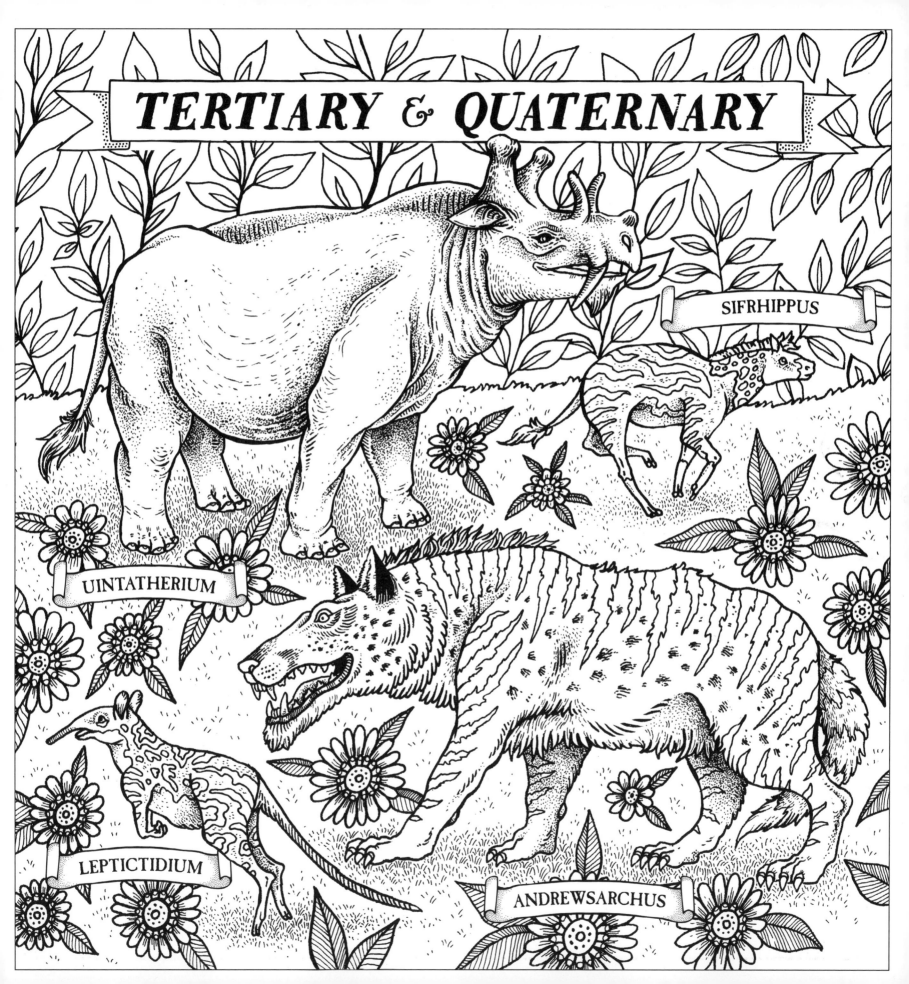

TERTIARY & QUATERNARY
66 million years ago – 2.6 million years ago – present day

After the mass extinction that occurred at the end of the Cretaceous Period (when as much as 80 percent of all species died out, including the dinosaurs), mammals, at last, began to thrive. During the Tertiary Period, the sizzling temperature dropped and sea levels subsided. Ice caps and glaciers formed at the polar regions again, and climates began to become more varied. Expansive grasslands spread across once-desolate land, and more and more animals ate grass for nourishment.

The Quaternary Period saw another shift in climate when the planet was plunged into another ice age. Glaciers covered up to 30 percent of the earth's surface, and ice flowed from the poles toward the equator. Random, warmer spells (known as "interglacials") interspersed this time, leading up to the present day, which is known as the Holocene Epoch.

UINTATHERIUM

Name translation: Beast from the Uinta Mountains
Diet: Roots, plants, and vegetables
Size: 13 ft (4 m)

This rhinoceros-like creature had unusual horns on its head and a pair of long fangs protruding down from its mouth. Experts believe that, despite their similar appearance, rhinos are in no way related to *Uintatherium*.

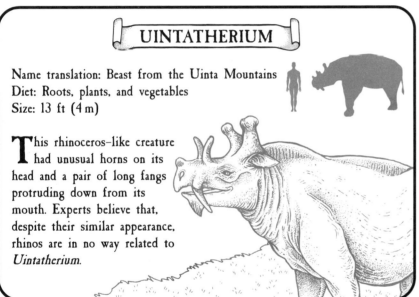

SIFRHIPPUS

Name translation: Hyrax beast
Diet: Leaves
Size: 24 in (60 cm)

Sifrhippus, also known as "dawn horse," was the first genus (type) of horse ever to exist. Unlike the horses we are familiar with today, *Sifrhippus* was tiny (roughly the same size as a cat).

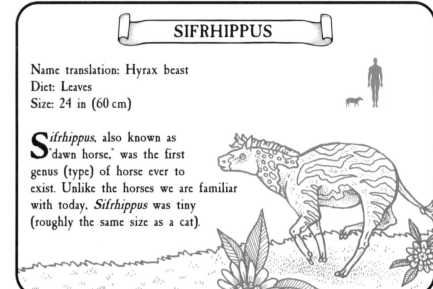

LEPTICTIDIUM

Name translation: Delicate weasel
Diet: Insects, small mammals, and small amphibians
Size: 35 in (90 cm)

Pristine *Leptictidium* fossils were found in a famous fossil pit in Germany, known as Messel Pit. The fur markings and stomach contents of the specimens were intact. Its large hind legs indicate it was a biped (two-footed), however, scientists are unsure if it hopped or walked.

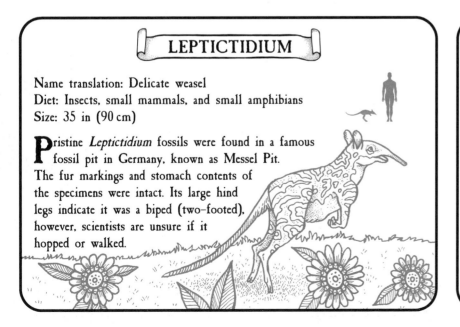

ANDREWSARCHUS

Name translation: Andrews' beast
Diet: Medium-sized mammals
Size: 13 ft (4 m)

One of the biggest carnivorous land mammals of all time, this grizzly-bear-sized beast was a dominant predator during the Early Tertiary Period. Its skull was 3 feet (1 meter) long, and its back teeth were built to chomp through gristle and bone.

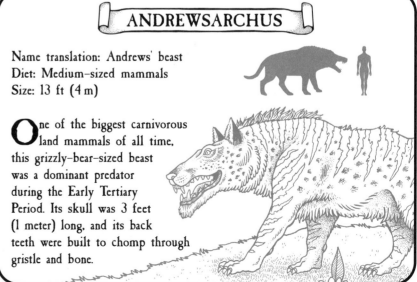

ODOBENOCETOPS

Name translation: Walrus-like whale
Diet: Worms and shellfish
Size: 7 ft (2 m)

Odobenocetops had two tusks (one sometimes much larger than the other), but no other teeth. It had to use its lips to suck and filter food from the seabed or from muddy embankments.

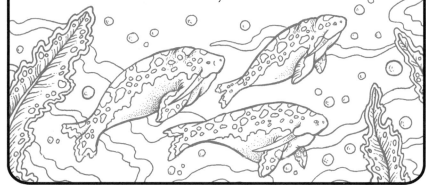

AMBULOCETUS

Name translation: Walking whale
Diet: Fish
Size: 10 ft (3 m)

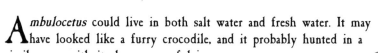

Ambulocetus could live in both salt water and fresh water. It may have looked like a furry crocodile, and it probably hunted in a similar way with its long, powerful jaws.

BASILOSAURUS

Name translation: Emperor lizard
Diet: Fish and squid
Size: 66 ft (20 m)

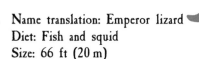

Basilosaurus had an extremely long and slender body, perfect for carving and cutting through the sea. When it was first discovered (in the mid-nineteenth century by an anatomist named Richard Harlan), experts thought that *Basilosaurus* was a reptile, which is why its name sounds like that of a dinosaur. *Basilosaurus* actually belonged to the whale family.

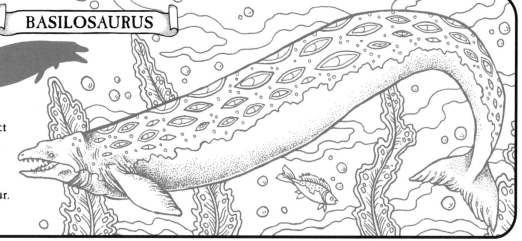

MEGALODON

Name translation: Big tooth
Diet: Whales and fish
Size: 49 ft (15 m)

More than two-and-a-half times the size of a great white shark, *Megalodon* had jaws so large that a fully-grown human could stand inside them. It is widely acknowledged that this giant species preyed on whales and other enormous ocean-dwelling animals. Some paleontologists even hypothesize that this massive shark may have grown to 66 feet (20 meters) in length, making *Megalodon* the biggest predator ever to exist.

AMEBELODON

Name translation: Shovel tooth
Diet: Plants
Size: 13 ft (4 m)

This animal's mandible (lower jawbone) was shaped like a shovel, making it the perfect tool for uprooting plants and scooping them into its mouth. The wear and tear on one specimen's tusks, however, suggests that *Amebelodon* may also have used its teeth to strip bark from trees and to dredge through mud in riverbeds in search of food.

TITANOBOA

Name translation: Titanic boa
Diet: Fish and other water-dwelling creatures
     (crocodiles, for example)
Size: 46 ft (14 m)

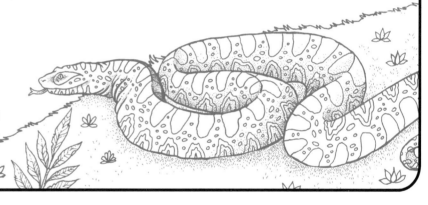

Titanoboa could weigh more than 2,200 pounds (1,000 kilograms) and was so large that it could engulf an alligator whole. The largest snakes alive on the planet today can only grow to approximately half the size of this dreaded beast. *Titanoboa* was not venomous. Instead, it constricted its prey, eventually suffocating its catch with a force so strong that it could break bones.

DINOHYUS

Name translation: Terrible pig
Diet: Carrion (decaying animals) and vegetation
Size: 10 ft (3 m)

Resembling an enormous warthog, with bony bumps and knobs projecting from its skull, *Dinohyus* stood as tall as a human and as large as a bison.

SYNTHETOCERAS

Name translation: Combined horn
Diet: Grass
Size: 7 ft (2 m)

Male *Synthetoceras* had a strange Y-shaped horn jutting from their noses. It is thought, therefore, that the males of the herd may have used the horns in some way when competing for dominance, in the same way that modern deer rut (compete for mates).

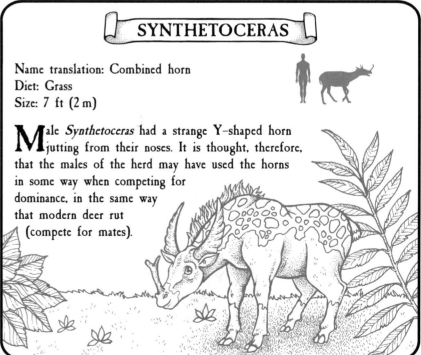

INDRICOTHERIUM

EMBOLOTHERIUM

INDRICOTHERIUM

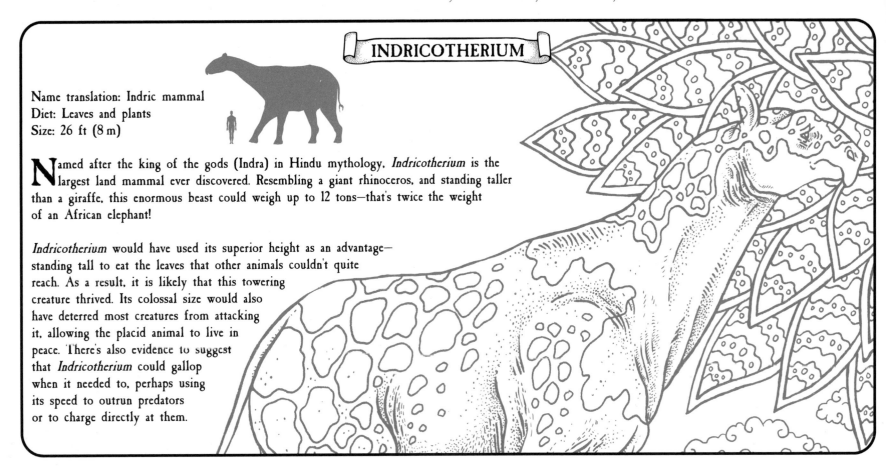

Name translation: Indric mammal
Diet: Leaves and plants
Size: 26 ft (8 m)

Named after the king of the gods (Indra) in Hindu mythology, *Indricotherium* is the largest land mammal ever discovered. Resembling a giant rhinoceros, and standing taller than a giraffe, this enormous beast could weigh up to 12 tons—that's twice the weight of an African elephant!

Indricotherium would have used its superior height as an advantage—standing tall to eat the leaves that other animals couldn't quite reach. As a result, it is likely that this towering creature thrived. Its colossal size would also have deterred most creatures from attacking it, allowing the placid animal to live in peace. There's also evidence to suggest that *Indricotherium* could gallop when it needed to, perhaps using its speed to outrun predators or to charge directly at them.

EMBOLOTHERIUM

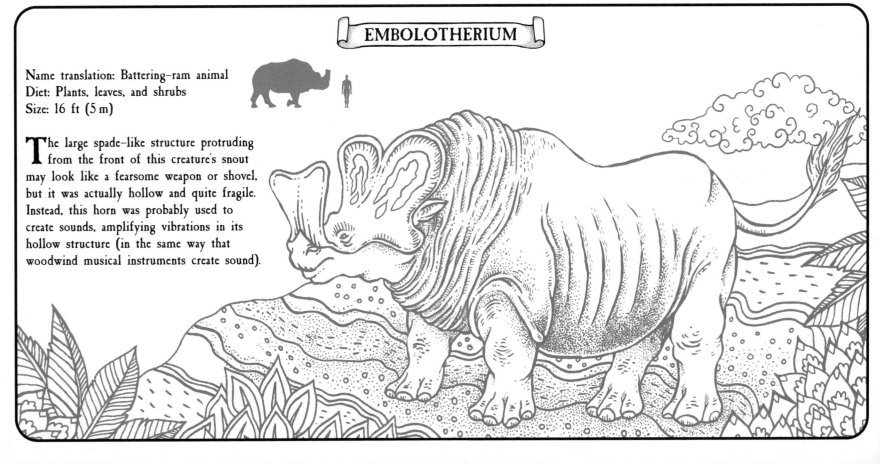

Name translation: Battering-ram animal
Diet: Plants, leaves, and shrubs
Size: 16 ft (5 m)

The large spade-like structure protruding from the front of this creature's snout may look like a fearsome weapon or shovel, but it was actually hollow and quite fragile. Instead, this horn was probably used to create sounds, amplifying vibrations in its hollow structure (in the same way that woodwind musical instruments create sound).

HARPAGORNIS

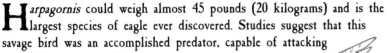

Name translation: Grappling-hook bird
Diet: Plant-eating animals
Size: 8 ft (2.5 m) wingspan

Harpagornis could weigh almost 45 pounds (20 kilograms) and is the largest species of eagle ever discovered. Studies suggest that this savage bird was an accomplished predator, capable of attacking and killing prey much bigger than itself. *Harpagornis* actively hunted *Dinornis*, for instance.

AEPYORNIS

Name translation: Tall bird
Diet: Fruits and seeds
Size: 10 ft (3 m) tall

Also known as the "elephant bird," *Aepyornis* could weigh as much as 1,100 pounds (500 kilograms), making it the heaviest bird ever to exist. It also produced the largest eggs, with some fossilized specimens measuring 3 feet (1 meter) in circumference.

Aepyornis lived on the island nation of Madagascar, off the east coast of Africa.

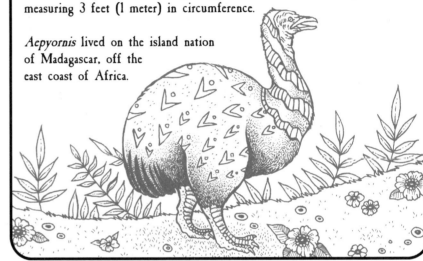

DINORNIS

Name translation: Terrible bird
Diet: Leaves, plants, and fruits
Size: 11.5 ft (3.5 m) tall

Dinornis is the tallest bird in history. Native to New Zealand, *Dinornis*, also called "moa," is believed by some scientists to have died out only 150–200 years ago.

TITANIS

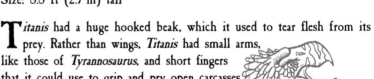

Name translation: Giant bird
Diet: Plant-eating animals and carrion
(decaying animals)
Size: 8.8 ft (2.7 m) tall

Titanis had a huge hooked beak, which it used to tear flesh from its prey. Rather than wings, *Titanis* had small arms, like those of *Tyrannosaurus*, and short fingers that it could use to grip and pry open carcasses.

GLYPTODON

MEGATHERIUM

DOEDICURUS

THALASSOCNUS

ACROPHOCA

GLYPTODON

Name translation: Carved tooth
Diet: Grass
Size: 10 ft (3 m)

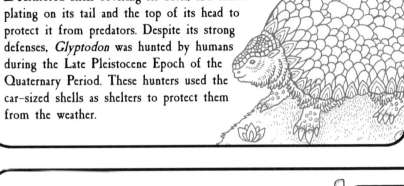

Resembling an armadillo, *Glyptodon* had an armored shell covering its back, and armor plating on its tail and the top of its head to protect it from predators. Despite its strong defenses, *Glyptodon* was hunted by humans during the Late Pleistocene Epoch of the Quaternary Period. These hunters used the car-sized shells as shelters to protect them from the weather.

MEGATHERIUM

Name translation: Giant mammal
Diet: Leaves (and possibly meat)
Size: 20 ft (6 m)

Megatherium had giant claws, which it used to dig and to strip trees and branches for food. It may also have used its claws as weapons. *Megatherium* belonged to the sloth family and was probably extremely slow and sluggish. It weighed as much as an elephant and often carried its colossal bulk on two legs.

DOEDICURUS

Name translation: Pestle tail
Diet: Grass
Size: 13 ft (4 m)

Doedicurus had a powerful tail that it used as a defensive weapon. It is thought that males competed for dominance by battering each other's shells with their mace-like tails. In fact, many shells have been discovered with indentations, scuffs, and scratches on them to support this theory.

THALASSOCNUS

Name translation: Sea sloth
Diet: Sea grass and plants
Size: 7 ft (2 m)

This giant sloth lived a semi-aquatic lifestyle, rummaging for plants and seaweed in the shallows. It had dense bones that helped it dive.

ACROPHOCA

Name translation: Extreme seal
Diet: Fish
Size: 5 ft (1.5 m)

With a long neck, slender tail, and sleek body, *Acrophoca* was perfectly streamlined and brilliantly adapted to a life chasing and catching fish. Modern seals are much bulkier because they require thick layers of fat to keep them warm in cold climates.

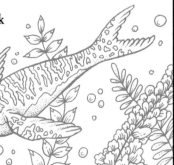

MAMMUTHUS

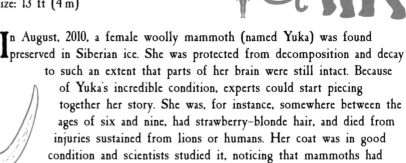

Name translation: Earth burrower
Diet: Bark, twigs, and leaves
Size: 13 ft (4 m)

In August, 2010, a female woolly mammoth (named Yuka) was found preserved in Siberian ice. She was protected from decomposition and decay to such an extent that parts of her brain were still intact. Because of Yuka's incredible condition, experts could start piecing together her story. She was, for instance, somewhere between the ages of six and nine, had strawberry-blonde hair, and died from injuries sustained from lions or humans. Her coat was in good condition and scientists studied it, noticing that mammoths had hair six times thicker than humans. Their outer layer of hair formed a long, dense coat, similar to that of a musk ox. This layer of hair helped protect the animals from the elements, providing a barrier against water and wind.

It is thought that mammoths died out when Earth's climate became too warm. Their extinction was probably also accelerated by early humans, who hunted the beasts, causing numbers to dwindle and eventually collapse.

COELODONTA

Name translation: Hollow tooth
Diet: Grass and other
low-growing plants
Size: 11.5 ft (3.5 m)

Coelodonta, also known as a "woolly rhino," had a 3-foot (1-meter) long horn on the top of its snout, with a short horn directly behind it. These horns were used for self-defense and made from a substance called keratin (the same material that is in our nails and hair).

Many woolly rhinos have been unearthed over the years. In 1929, for example, in an area of Ukraine called Starunia, the remains of a preserved female *Coelodonta* were discovered with the internal organs and skin still intact. Also, in 2007, a specimen was discovered near a gold mine entrance. Experts analyzed the creature, observing that its squat and stocky build may have eventually led to its downfall. As snowfall became more frequent in the Quaternary Period, snowdrifts got deeper and deeper. Woolly rhinos would have had immense trouble crossing such terrain. They were simply too heavy to float on top of snow, and it is likely that huge numbers died from exhaustion and starvation.